Words You Deserve to Hear

Sage Liberty

Ukiyoto Publishing

All global publishing rights are held by

Ukiyoto Publishing

Published in 2025

Content Copyright © Sage Liberty

ISBN 9789370091191

All rights reserved.
No part of this publication may be reproduced, transmitted, or stored in a retrieval system, in any form by any means, electronic, mechanical, photocopying, recording or otherwise, without the prior permission of the publisher.

The moral rights of the author have been asserted.

This is a work of fiction. Names, characters, businesses, places, events, locales, and incidents are either the products of the author's imagination or used in a fictitious manner. Any resemblance to actual persons, living or dead, or actual events is purely coincidental.

This book is sold subject to the condition that it shall not by way of trade or otherwise, be lent, resold, hired out or otherwise circulated, without the publisher's prior consent, in any form of binding or cover other than that in which it is published.

www.ukiyoto.com

Dedication

There comes a point in life where you stop and think: *Is this it?*

Where everyone else seems to be moving forward. Getting their lives together, glowing up, achieving milestones, while you're stuck, questioning everything.

I've been there.

This book is for the ones who feel too much and speak too little. The ones who push through each day with silent battles no one knows about. It's for the overthinkers, the late bloomers, the dreamers, and the tired hearts.

No matter what stage you're in—trying to love yourself, chasing your goals, healing from pain, or just figuring things out—I hope this book feels like a warm hug and a little nudge forward.

I won't pretend to have all the answers. I'm not a guru or a therapist. I'm just someone who's lived through the questions, felt the confusion, and found pieces of peace along the way. This is a mix of my personal experiences and honest advice that I hope resonates with you.

Each chapter in this book focuses on a specific theme. You don't have to read it in order. Go where your heart needs healing.

And if there's one thing I want you to take from all of this, it's that you are not behind, and you are not alone. Life doesn't have a strict timeline. You're not late.

You're just living at your own pace—and that is perfectly okay.

This book, contains the words you deserve to hear.

Contents

Chapter 1: Self-Love	1
The Quiet Revolution	1
Chapter 2: Productivity Without Burnout	4
Getting Things Done Without Losing Yourself	4
Chapter 3: Healing from Heartbreak	7
When The Pieces Don't Fit Anymore	7
Chapter 4: Building Confidence	12
Learning to Stand Tall, Even When You Shake	12
Chapter 5: Managing Anxiety	17
Learning To Breathe Through The Storm	17
Chapter 6: The Pain Of Being Left Behind	20
Finding Yourself After They Walk Away	20
Chapter 7: Building Better Habits	24
Becoming Who You Want To Be, One Small Step At A Time	24
Chapter 8: The Journey of Self-Discovery	29
Meeting The Real You Beneath The Noise	29
Chapter 9: You Are Not Alone	35
A Letter to Anyone Who's Still Healing	35
A Letter To You, The Reader	39
ABOUT THE AUTHOR	*40*

Chapter 1: Self-Love
The Quiet Revolution

Self-love.

It's a word that gets thrown around so often that it starts to lose its meaning. You see it everywhere—on Instagram posts, in morning mantras, printed on coffee mugs. "Love yourself," they say. But no one really explains *how* or *why* it's so hard.

Here's the truth: self-love isn't always soft and sweet. It's not always rainbows and sunshines. Sometimes, it's messy and dark. Sometimes, it's choosing to forgive yourself when you really, really don't want to. Sometimes, it's looking in the mirror and choosing not to criticize the reflection, even if your mind tries to.

Self-love is a quiet, daily practice. It's waking up and deciding, even on the hardest days, that you are still worthy of kindness, even if it only comes from you. We often think self-love must look loud. But sometimes, it's silent. It's choosing to rest instead of pushing yourself to the brink. It's admitting you're tired. It's walking away from things that hurt, even when they once made you feel alive.

Many of us didn't always love ourselves. In fact, I didn't even like myself for a long time. I used to think that if I worked hard enough, looked good enough, or achieved enough, then I'd finally be worthy. But no matter how many wins I got, there was always an echoing voice saying, "You're still not enough."

Maybe you've heard that voice too.

Self-love is how you show up for yourself even when the world tells you you're not worth the effort. It's more than a feeling. It's an action. A choice.

Start by talking to yourself like someone you love. Would you call your best friend ugly, lazy, or a failure? No? Then don't do that to yourself.

Instead of "I'm so stupid," try "I'm still learning."

Instead of "I look terrible," try "I'm more than my appearance."

Celebrate yourself, not just for achievements, but for your existence. You matter. You always have.

Saying "no" is an act of love. Please, please, create your boundaries. You don't have to attend every event, respond to every message, or please everyone. Protect your peace. You don't need to achieve something really big to be proud of yourself. Getting out of bed on a hard day is worth celebrating too. You're allowed to take breaks. You're allowed to outgrow things. You're allowed to change your mind. Loving yourself means giving yourself permission to be human.

Self-love is not, and will be never be selfish. This is important: loving yourself doesn't mean ignoring others. It doesn't mean becoming arrogant or self-obsessed. It means recognizing that you can't pour from an empty cup. You can't show up for anyone else if you're constantly abandoning yourself.

You deserve love—even from yourself. Especially from yourself.

Because at the end of the day, you're the one person who's going to be with you through every high and low, every messy middle, every beautiful beginning. Don't make your own mind your own enemy.

The relationship you have with yourself is the foundation for everything else.

How you speak to yourself in the dark, how you hold yourself together when things fall apart, this is the kind of love that carries you. You don't need to earn it. You were never meant to beg for it. You just need to believe, little by little, that you are enough, even in your mess.

Stop chasing perfection. It's a myth. Embrace your flaws, your softness, your strength, your stumbles. Every version of you deserves love. Every version is trying. Growth doesn't always look like progress. Sometimes it looks like sitting in stillness and listening to what your heart needs.

You are allowed to grow slowly. You are allowed to say no. These are not signs of weakness; they are signs of deep self-respect. Don't silence your needs to make others comfortable. Don't water yourself down to fit into someone else's mold.

So be gentle with yourself. Be patient. There's no rush to become a better version of you—you are already someone worth loving, exactly as you are.

Watch what happens when you start choosing you.

Chapter 2: Productivity Without Burnout
Getting Things Done Without Losing Yourself

Let's get this straight: you don't get to be busy 24/7 to be valuable.

Somewhere along the line, we were taught that if we aren't constantly *doing*, then we're falling behind. That if we rest, we're wasting time. That unless we're always productive, we don't deserve to feel proud of ourselves. You push yourself beyond your limits just to feel "enough." You sacrifice sleep, meals, and rest just to meet expectations, often ones you didn't even set for yourself. And when you couldn't keep up, you felt like a failure. And in the end? You're exhausted, unmotivated, maybe even bitter.

We live in a world that glorifies being busy. Where your worth often feels tied to how much you accomplish in a day. But productivity without rest is a slow path to burnout. And burnout doesn't always announce itself. It creeps in quietly. You begin to feel exhausted, but you keep pushing. You lose excitement for things you once loved. You feel guilty for resting. Eventually, your body whispers what your mind tries to ignore: you need to stop.

Burnout is one of the worst feelings out there. It's constant fatigue no matter how much you sleep, losing motivation for things you once loved, becoming easily irritated or numb, and feeling like you're never doing enough, even when you're overworking. If that sounds like you, pause. You're not lazy, you're drained. And that's not a flaw. This is your sign to slow down. Not quit, not give up. Just slow down.

Busy isn't always better. Just because your day is full doesn't mean it's fulfilling. Just because you're tired doesn't mean you were productive. And just because everyone else is grinding doesn't mean you need to burn yourself out to keep up.

You don't owe the world a total burnout to prove your ambition. You are not a machine. You are not made to function endlessly without care. True productivity includes breaks. It includes pausing. It includes saying, "I've done enough for today." Productivity means nothing if you're miserable. I learned that the hard way.

Real productivity isn't about doing *more*. It's about doing what *matters*. Sometimes that's finishing a big project. Other times, it's doing laundry, taking a nap, or letting yourself cry. You're allowed to call those things productive too. Both are valid. Both are productive. True productivity comes with clarity, not chaos.

Start with using the "3-Task Rule"

Each day, pick:

1 major task (e.g., finish a report)

1 minor task (e.g., reply to emails)

1 personal task (e.g., go for a walk)

Track energy, not just time. Notice when you feel most energized (morning? Late night?). Do your hardest tasks then. Match your work with your energy, not the clock. Give each task its time. Don't try to write an essay while replying to messages and watching YouTube. Your brain isn't built for that. And most importantly, *rest*. Not "scroll on the phone" rest. Don't wait until you crash. Walk. Stretch. Breathe. Listen to music. Or just do nothing. You're allowed.

Remember: you are more than what you produce. Your value isn't tied to how much you get done. You're not a machine. You're allowed to move slow. You're allowed to have off days. You're allowed to just be. Give yourself permission to exist outside of hustle. You can be productive and gentle with yourself. You can chase dreams and rest without guilt. You can be productive without losing your peace. You're not supposed to carry everything alone. Delegate. Delay. Delete what isn't urgent. The world won't end if you slow down.

You are not what you do. You are how you care. How you show up for yourself when no one is watching. And sometimes, the most productive thing you can do is give yourself permission to pause.

You're still worthy, even when you're resting. Rest isn't something you "earn." It's something you need. And it doesn't make you weak. It makes you wise.

You're doing better than you think.

Chapter 3: Healing from Heartbreak
When The Pieces Don't Fit Anymore

No one really prepares you for the kind of silence that follows heartbreak. It's not just about the person being gone. It's about the memories and the future you imagined with them vanishing too. It's waking up and reaching for someone who's no longer there. It's re-learning how to exist without them in your everyday life.

And the hardest part?

It's not always a clean break. Sometimes you still love them. Sometimes you don't even hate them. And sometimes you hate that you don't.

Heartbreak can come in many forms: losing a partner, a friend, a dream, even a version of yourself. Whatever shape it takes, the pain is real. It lingers in the little things: in songs, in scents, in places you used to go together.

I've been there. I've sat with tears I couldn't explain, scrolled through old photos knowing I shouldn't, and asked myself, "Why wasn't I enough?"

Heartbreak doesn't just shatter you. It reshapes you. It changes the way you see love, trust, and sometimes even yourself. Healing from heartbreak is not about pretending it didn't hurt. It's about learning how to breathe through the ache. It's about waking up each day with a little less heaviness in your chest, even if it's just by an inch.

If you're here, if you're hurting, then this chapter is for you.

Let Yourself Feel Everything

The worst thing you can do after a heartbreak is rush your healing. Don't force yourself to be okay. You don't need to bounce back in a week, or pretend it didn't hurt. Let it hurt. Let it ache. Grief isn't a weakness. It's proof that you cared deeply. Cry if you need to. Write letters you'll never send. Let the emotions come, wave after wave. You don't have to be strong all the time. Let yourself grieve. Not just the person, but the version of your life you imagined with them. The shared plans, the familiar laughter, the comfort of being known. You are allowed to miss them and still move forward. You are allowed to cry one moment and laugh the next.

It wasn't all your fault. Read that again.

It's easy to replay the memories and wonder what you could've done differently. But relationships end for many reasons, and most of them have nothing to do with your worth.

Sometimes timing is wrong.

Sometimes people grow apart.

Sometimes someone simply doesn't know how to love you the way you deserve.

That doesn't make you unlovable.

That doesn't mean you'll never find love again.

Healing isn't linear. You'll have days where you feel free, and days where a song shatters you. Both days are part of the process.

It's okay to unfollow, block, mute or whatever gives you peace. Healing requires space. You don't need to stay in touch just to prove you're mature. Don't bottle it up. Vent to a friend, a journal, a therapist. Speak your pain so it doesn't rot inside.

And lastly, forgive yourself.

Forgive yourself for not seeing the red flags.

Forgive yourself for staying too long.

Forgive yourself for hoping it would change.

You Did Your Best For The Love You Had

The truth is, some people leave, not because you are unworthy of love, but because their chapter in your story has ended. And even though it hurts, there's peace in knowing that not everyone is meant to stay. Sometimes, people are just lessons in disguise, teaching you what you want, what you need, and most importantly, what you deserve.

As you heal, remember this: you are not broken. Your ability to love deeply is not a flaw—it's your strength. Don't let pain harden your heart. Let it refine your boundaries. Let it guide you back to yourself. This heartbreak is not the end of your story. It's the middle. And beautiful things can grow here, too.

Surround yourself with people who hold space for your sadness without trying to rush you through it. Write letters you'll never send. Go on walks that lead nowhere. Reconnect with the parts of yourself that got lost in loving someone else. Little by little, you will feel like you again.

You won't forget them entirely, and that's okay. But one day, their name won't sting. One day, your heart will feel light again. And when that day comes, you'll be proud, not just because you survived, but because you chose to keep loving, living, and showing up, even when it was hard.

You're not healing to be ready for someone else. You're healing for you. Because you deserve a heart that feels whole, even if no one is holding it but you.

You Will Love Again (And Be Loved Right)

Sometimes, the pain from your past love makes it hard to believe that anything better could exist. But just because someone couldn't love you right doesn't mean no one will. There is love out there that won't make you question your worth. Love that won't punish you for being too soft, too much, or too honest. You won't have to beg for it. You won't have to shrink for it.

The right kind of love will feel like calm, not chaos. It won't come with mixed signals or silence as punishment. It will choose you. Consistently, kindly, and clearly. It will make room for your emotions, your needs, and your dreams. It will celebrate your growth and support your healing.

But first, you have to believe you're worthy of that kind of love. You have to stop settling for halves when you've always deserved wholes. Let go of the idea that love should hurt to be real. It shouldn't. Real love doesn't leave you guessing. It doesn't leave you empty.

The person meant for you will meet you where you are. They won't be perfect, and neither will you. But the love will be honest. And mutual. And safe.

Right now, it might feel like no one else could ever understand you the way they did. Like no one else will ever make your heart race like that again. But love returns, in different forms, in softer ways, in people who choose you without hesitation.

Until then, focus on you. Build a life you love so deeply that someone else becomes a beautiful addition, not a missing piece. You are already whole.

Don't settle for someone who only loved the easy parts of you. Wait for the one who stays for the hard parts, too.

And in the meantime? Love yourself like they didn't.

I know this hurts. But I promise you, you will feel whole again.

Chapter 4: Building Confidence
Learning to Stand Tall, Even When You Shake

Confidence isn't about always having the right words. Or walking into a room with your head held high and thinking you're better than everyone else.

It's about walking into a room and not needing to compare yourself to anyone at all. It's about trusting that even when your voice shakes, it still matters. It's believing that your presence alone is worth something, even before you prove a single thing.

But let's be real. Confidence doesn't come naturally for everyone. Some of us were raised in environments where we were constantly doubted, criticized, or overlooked. Some of us learned to shrink ourselves just to keep the peace. And some of us have been carrying the weight of "not good enough" for way too long. So if you struggle with confidence, I get it. You're not alone. And it's not your fault.

But here's the beautiful part: confidence can be built. Slowly. Gently. With practice, patience, and a whole lot of self-forgiveness.

You Don't Need To Be Fearless To Feel Confident

We often think confidence shows up only when we feel ready, but sometimes it's built in the moments when we feel most uncertain. It's choosing to try anyway. It's stepping forward even when doubt tugs at your sleeves. Every small act of courage, every time you speak up, every time you stand your ground, adds a brick to your foundation.

Confidence is born from showing up despite the fear. It's knowing that failure doesn't define you. It teaches you. You can stumble and still be powerful. You can be unsure and still move forward. Confidence is less about the absence of insecurity and more about your willingness to keep going anyway.

Start by speaking gently to yourself. Confidence blooms when the inner critic quiets down. Replace "I can't" with "I'm learning." Trade "I'm not enough" for "I'm growing." Shift your mindset, and the world around you begins to shift too.

Be proud of how far you've come. Celebrate the boldness it takes to show up in a world that constantly tries to mold you. Let your confidence be soft, honest, and rooted in who you are—not who the world expects you to be.

Where Insecurities Comes From

Insecurities often don't originate from who we are, but from what we're told we should be. Society, media, and sometimes even people close to us project their expectations, shaping our perception of ourselves. We're made to feel as though we need to meet certain standards—whether it's body image, success, or even how we express our emotions. When we don't fit these molds, we start to question our worth.

Insecurity grows from the seeds of comparison, failure, rejection, and fear.

Sometimes it's a voice from your past. A parent who never encouraged you. A teacher who embarrassed you. A partner who made you feel small.

But you don't have to carry those voices with you forever. You get to rewrite the narrative.

Recognizing where insecurities stem from is the first step in reclaiming your power. You can challenge those beliefs. You can redefine your worth on your own terms, not by someone else's standards. You are whole, worthy, and enough, regardless of where these insecurities may have come from.

Confidence isn't pretending those wounds don't exist.

It's choosing to grow anyway.

Confidence Isn't Loud. It's Honest

You don't need to be the most outspoken person in the room to be confident.

Confidence is quiet assurance. It's choosing to show up as yourself without apology.

It's saying:

"I don't know yet, but I'm willing to learn."

"I deserve to be here, even if I'm still figuring things out."

"I am enough, just as I am."

True confidence isn't loud. It doesn't boast. It's quiet but steady. It's rooted in the understanding that you are allowed to take up space exactly as you are.

Start cutting off those people who bring negativity to your life and start surrounding yourself with safe people because the right people won't dim your light. They'll hype you up when you forget how bright you are. Find those people. Be that person for others too.

Confidence isn't built through compliments from others. It's built by proving to yourself that you can be trusted. If you say you'll show up, show up. Even for the little things.

Step out from your comfort zone *gently*. Do one thing a week that scares you just a little. Raise your hand. Speak up. Try something new. Every small win stacks up.

Look back, not just forward. You've already survived hard things. You've already grown in ways you didn't think you could. Let your past resilience remind you how capable you truly are.

You Don't Need to Be "Fixed" to Be Confident

Confidence is not born in perfection. It grows in acceptance. The more you try to "fix" yourself into someone else's version of ideal, the further you drift from your truth. You are not a problem to be solved. You are a person to be embraced.

The world profits off your insecurities. It sells you creams, routines, and rules you never asked for, convincing you that you must be more. More polished, more beautiful, more successful—before you can truly believe in yourself. But confidence is quiet rebellion. It's choosing to show up fully, even when you've been taught to hide.

You don't need to erase your scars, your quirks, your softness. You don't need to silence your emotions or pretend to have it all together. Confidence doesn't require perfection; it requires honesty. It starts when you decide to show up as yourself, without apology.

You don't need perfect skin, a perfect body, or a perfect life. You don't need to "have it all together." Confidence doesn't come after you achieve things. It comes from believing you're already worthy, even while you're still growing.

You are not behind. You are not broken. You are not waiting to be fixed. You are learning, unfolding, and becoming—and that is more than enough to stand tall.

You're allowed to be a work in progress and still be proud of who you are.

Every step forward counts. Even the wobbly ones.

Chapter 5: Managing Anxiety Learning To Breathe Through The Storm

Anxiety doesn't always look like panic attacks or heavy breathing. It is not always loud. Sometimes, it's a quiet hum in the background—a tightening in your chest, racing thoughts, or the urge to escape your own mind. And while it may feel like a personal flaw, it's not. Anxiety is a response, not a weakness.

Sometimes it's overthinking every text you send, imagining the worst-case scenario out of habit, and being exhausted from doing absolutely nothing because your brain's been running marathons all day.

If this sounds like you, you're not alone. Anxiety is more common than we admit, and it doesn't make you weak. It makes you *human*.

Maybe you've had days where even opening your messages felt like climbing a mountain. Maybe you've canceled plans you were excited about because suddenly, your chest felt too heavy. And maybe you've smiled through the day while quietly drowning on the inside.

So, if you've ever felt like that, let me tell you this:

You are not broken. You are not crazy. And you are not alone.

Anxiety Isn't the Enemy

Anxiety is your body's alarm system. It's trying to protect you.

But sometimes, it misfires.

It mistakes a job interview, a social gathering, or even a text message as a threat. And suddenly, your heart races. Your hands shake. Your thoughts spiral.

The goal isn't to shut off anxiety completely. It's to learn how to turn down the volume when it gets too loud.

You don't need to fight your anxiety like it's the enemy. Sometimes, the most powerful thing you can do is sit with it gently, without judgment. Ask it what it's trying to say.. Anxiety often carries stories, fears, and past wounds that haven't yet been healed. Listening doesn't mean agreeing—it just means acknowledging its presence.

Some things you can do to help you pull out of your thoughts and back into the present is putting your thoughts into words. It will make them less overwhelming.

This technique is called box breathing:

Inhale for 4 seconds.

Hold it for 4 seconds.

Exhale for 4 seconds.

You can also try 5-4-3-2-1 technique:

5 things you can see.

4 things you can touch.

3 things you can hear.

2 things you can smell.

1 thing you can taste.

You Are Not a Burden

Anxiety can make you feel like you're "too much."

Too emotional. Too sensitive. Too fragile.

But here's the truth: the people who truly love you will not think less of you because you're anxious. They'll stand beside you in the storm. And they'll remind you: you are still lovable, even when your mind is in chaos.

You are not your anxious thoughts. They may feel real, but they are not always true. You can observe them without absorbing them. Let them pass through you like waves—not holding on, just letting go.

Take care of your nervous system. Rest. Move your body. Drink water. Set boundaries. Speak kindly to yourself when your anxiety flares. You are not failing. You're simply being human.

Anxiety doesn't define you. You can still be strong, successful, and kind even when you're shaking. You can still show up, even with a nervous heart. And every time you do, you are proving to yourself that you can live fully even with fear.

You are not your anxiety.

You are so *much more*.

You are safe. You are doing your best. You don't have to figure everything out today. One breathe at a time.

Chapter 6: The Pain Of Being Left Behind
Finding Yourself After They Walk Away

There's a particular ache in being the one who stays.

The one who watches people leave.

Friends drifting apart. A lover choosing someone else. People forgetting the promises they once swore they'd keep.

Being left behind feels like a quiet ache that sits deep in your chest. It's the sting of watching someone move on without you, whether it's a relationship, a friendship, or even a dream that once included you. The pain often isn't loud; it's a dull, persistent throb that reminds you of what you've lost.

It hurts in a way that's hard to explain.

It's not just sadness. It's emptiness. It's silence. It's wondering if you were ever really enough for someone to stay.

If you've ever felt this way: abandoned, replaced, forgotten, then this chapter is for you.

Let's Be Honest: It Sucks

It sucks to watch people move on while you're still picking up the pieces.

It sucks to see someone you cared about smiling in new photos, while you're still crying over old ones.

It sucks to feel like you're easy to leave.

But I promise you, you are not disposable.

People leave for many reasons, and not all of them have anything to do with your worth.

The pain of being left behind comes from attachment, from the belief that something or someone outside of you defines your happiness. But you are whole on your own. You are not dependent on another person's presence to be complete. Healing from this pain means learning to find validation within yourself, not from others. It means remembering that your value is inherent, not conditional on someone else's choices.

Being Left Isn't a Reflection of Your Value

Maybe they changed.

Maybe you grew and they didn't.

Maybe they didn't know how to love you the way you needed.

Maybe they loved you, but not enough to stay through the hard parts.

Whatever the reason, they left. And it *wasn't* your fault.

You are still worthy of love, even if someone else couldn't give it.

You are still enough, even if they didn't see it.

You can and will love again. You can and will grow. You are more than what you've lost, and in time, the pain will transform into wisdom.

Being left behind doesn't define you—it refines you.

Let yourself grieve. Don't minimize it. Being left hurts. Grieve the loss. Cry. Scream. Journal. Do what you need to release it.

Don't chase closure that will never come. Sometimes people leave without explanation. Without a goodbye. Without the decency you deserved.

And as unfair as that is, chasing answers won't always bring peace.

Choose to give yourself closure: *"They left, and I will still heal."*

It's important to give yourself space to grieve the loss. Feel it fully. Let yourself be sad, angry, confused. These emotions are all valid. But also remember that just because something or someone is no longer in your life doesn't mean it's the end. The door may be closed, but it's only opening you up to new opportunities, new people, and new ways of being.

When people leave, we often lose parts of ourselves in the process.

Now is your time to remember:

What do you love? What brings you peace?

Start pouring love into the places they left empty.

It's easy to shut down your heart. To say, "Never again." But don't let one person's choice rob the world of the love only you can give.

Protect your heart, yes. But don't bury it.

Your People Are Still Out There

Not everyone will leave.

Not everyone will treat you like an option.

There are people—beautiful, real, genuine people who will show up, stay, and choose you again and again.

Not everyone will understand you, but those who do will see the beauty in your flaws and the strength in your vulnerability. The right people don't need you to be perfect—they just need you to be real. They will appreciate you for exactly who you are, and not for who you could become or who they want you to be. They will love you, even when you're not at your best.

There's comfort in knowing that not all relationships are meant to last forever, but that doesn't mean those moments weren't meaningful. Sometimes, the people who leave teach us the most about ourselves and what we truly need from others. Those lessons are valuable and necessary for the growth that comes next.

You haven't met all the people who will love you yet.

Until then, stay.

Stay for yourself.

Stay for the version of you that's still becoming.

Stay because you deserve to be here. Even when others walk away.

And when you do meet them, you'll realize that every moment, every challenge, and every heartbreak led you exactly to this point—right where you're meant to be.

Keep your heart open. Gently.

Chapter 7: Building Better Habits
Becoming Who You Want To Be, One Small Step At A Time

We all want to grow.

We dream of waking up earlier, being more productive, staying consistent with workouts, reading more, worrying less, eating better… the list goes on. But wanting to change and knowing how to change are two different things.

The truth is: becoming the person you want to be doesn't happen overnight. It's not about a grand transformation or a dramatic shift. It's about showing up, day after day, making choices that align with your vision for yourself. Change doesn't require perfection, only progress. Every small step forward, no matter how insignificant it may seem, is still a step in the right direction.

We become them slowly. Through tiny choices, repeated consistently.

One small change, one positive habit, one kind word to yourself can create a ripple effect. Over time, those small steps compound into something bigger, something you can be proud of. It's easy to get discouraged by the distance between where you are and where you want to be, but remember: transformation is built on consistency.

Take your time. You don't have to rush. You're already on your way, and every step you take brings you closer to the person you're meant to be.

Habits are the quiet builders of your future.

And whether you realize it or not, you already have habits. Some are helping you. Others... not so much. But here's the good news: you're in charge. You have the power to shift your habits and, in doing so, shift your life.

Why Habits Matter More Than Motivation

Motivation can be fleeting. Some days, you wake up feeling inspired, ready to conquer the world. Other days, it's nowhere to be found. It comes and goes.

That's where habits come in.

Habits are what keep you moving when motivation disappears. But habits? Habits are what carry you through on the days when motivation is absent. They are the quiet, dependable actions that keep you moving forward even when you don't feel like it.

They're the "autopilot" systems your brain uses to make life easier, and you can reprogram that autopilot to work for you instead of against you.

The beauty of habits is that they don't rely on motivation. You don't have to wait until you feel "in the mood" to work on your goals. When something becomes a habit, it becomes automatic. You don't have to convince yourself to do it, and you don't need the energy of motivation to get started. It simply becomes part of who you are.

Motivation is often the spark, but habits are the fire that keeps burning. When you rely on habits, you create a sustainable path toward progress, no matter how motivated you feel.

Start Small. Really Small.

Most people fail at building habits because they go too big, too fast.

You don't need to run 5k on day one. Start with a 10-minute walk.

Don't try to read a whole book. Start with two pages.

Don't cut out all sugar. Start by swapping one drink for water.

Make the habit hard to miss by keeping your goal simple. Make the first step so small you *can't* say no.

Celebrate your wins, even the small ones. Your brain likes pleasure. Attach good feelings to your habits.

Progress > perfection.

Consistency > intensity.

Breaking Bad Habits

Breaking bad habits is often harder than we expect because they've become ingrained in our daily routine. The familiarity of a bad habit makes it feel comforting, even though it's doing more harm than good. But just because a habit feels easy doesn't mean it's helping you grow. The first step in breaking any bad habit is awareness. Recognize that it doesn't serve you anymore and that you're worthy of making better choices. Once you have that awareness, you can begin to challenge your patterns.

We all have habits we want to unlearn. Doom-scrolling, procrastinating, self-sabotaging, overthinking. Breaking them starts with awareness, not shame.

Ask yourself:

What's the trigger?

What need am I trying to meet?

Is there a better way to meet that need?

Replace the bad with something healthier. Not perfect, just better.

You Don't Have to Be Disciplined. Just Consistent

Discipline can feel like an overwhelming, unattainable goal—something only certain people are born with. But consistency? That's something we can all achieve. Consistency doesn't require you to be perfect, nor does it demand that you push yourself to your limits every single day. Instead, it's about showing up for yourself regularly, even when you're not feeling your best. It's the simple act of continuing, no matter how small your efforts may seem.

It's easy to get caught up in the myth that success comes from bursts of intense focus and willpower. But true progress comes from the slow, steady accumulation of effort. The key to consistency is not trying to go all in at once, but making sure you do a little bit each day. Whether it's writing a paragraph a day, taking a short walk, or practicing a new skill for just ten minutes, those moments add up over time.

When you focus on the process rather than the result, you find that consistency becomes its own reward.

You don't need superhuman willpower.

You need a system that supports the version of you you're becoming.

Missed a day? It's okay. Just don't miss two in a row.

Slipped up? You're human. Keep going. Progress isn't ruined by one off day.

Healing doesn't mean forgetting. It means remembering without breaking.

Chapter 8: The Journey of Self-Discovery
Meeting The Real You Beneath The Noise

Do you ever feel like you're living someone else's life? Like the person you see in the mirror isn't the one you truly know? That's because the real you is buried under layers of noise—expectations, fears, past experiences, and outside influences that cloud your vision of who you really are. The truth is, the more noise you listen to, the further you drift from the person you're meant to be.

The process isn't always easy. It can be messy and uncomfortable to confront the parts of yourself you've hidden or ignored. But it's necessary. Because only when you shed the masks and stop performing for others can you truly begin to understand your deepest desires, your passions, and what truly makes you feel alive.

You are not defined by the surface-level things that change over time. You are not just your career, your achievements, or your relationships. You are the sum of everything you've experienced, but also the quiet, authentic you that persists underneath. And once you embrace that version of yourself, you'll find a deeper sense of peace, purpose, and confidence that no external validation can provide.

So, the next time you're alone, ask yourself:

Who are you, really?

Not your job title. Not your grades. Not your relationship status.

Not the version of yourself you feel pressured to perform.

Who are you when the world gets quiet?

When the mask comes off?

When no one's watching?

That's what self-discovery is about.

It's not about "finding yourself" like you're some lost object.

It's about remembering who you've always been beneath everything you were told to be.

Why We Lose Ourselves

Sometimes we get so caught up in pleasing others, meeting expectations, and surviving day-to-day life that we forget to check in with ourselves.

We lose ourselves because we're taught that who we are isn't enough. Society, family, and even friends sometimes unknowingly push us toward an image of who we should be—an ideal version that fits neatly into what's expected of us. From a young age, we're conditioned to prioritize other people's needs and desires over our own. We're told that success looks a certain way, that happiness is found in achievements, and that our worth is determined by external validation.

As a result, we start to shape our identity based on these external pressures. We put on masks to fit in, to please, or to avoid rejection. Slowly, the authentic parts of ourselves get buried under expectations, self-doubt, and the constant striving to meet the standards of others. We forget that our value isn't determined by how well we fit into a mold. We forget that it's okay to stand out, to be different, to be ourselves.

We play roles. The Good Student. The Reliable Friend. The Strong One. The Overachiever.

And one day, we look in the mirror and think, "Wait… who even am I?"

That moment isn't a failure. It's an invitation.

An invitation to come home to yourself.

Self-Discovery Isn't Always Pretty, But It's Always Worth It

Getting to know yourself can feel messy.

You'll uncover beliefs that were never really yours.

You'll realize you've been living by rules that don't actually serve you.

You might even grieve the version of yourself you thought you had to be.

But it's in that unraveling that the truth starts to shine through.

When you dig deep into who you are, you often uncover things you'd rather not face. Old wounds, buried fears, and unresolved emotions can rise to the surface. It's tempting to shy away from these uncomfortable truths, but doing so only prolongs the healing process. Embracing the rawness of self-discovery allows you to break free from the limitations you've placed on yourself and start living in alignment with your true essence.

Reclaiming ourselves is about saying no to the things that don't align with our true nature and yes to what feels authentic, no matter how unconventional or unexpected it may be. It's about giving ourselves permission to be who we are, not who the world tells us to be.

Start Reconnecting With Yourself

Ask yourself a deep honest question:

What makes me feel alive?

What drains my energy?

When do I feel most like myself?

What would I do if no one judged me?

These questions are not just for reflection; they are invitations to rediscover what truly matters to you. So often, we get caught up in the noise and expectations of the world that we forget to check in with ourselves. We forget to ask the hard questions that lead us back to who we really are. By taking the time to sit with these questions, you create space to connect with the deepest parts of yourself—those parts that are often drowned out by the busyness of life.

Spend time alone (and not just scrolling.) Being alone doesn't mean being lonely. It's in these moments of solitude that you can truly hear your own thoughts, your own desires. It's an opportunity to listen to your inner voice without distractions.

Try new things without expecting perfection. You don't have to be great at it. You just have to be curious and explore. When you try new things without the pressure of perfection, you open yourself up to the possibility of growth. You allow yourself to be a beginner again, to explore without judgment, and to experience life with fresh eyes.

Write without editing yourself. Write like no one will read it. Be honest. Be raw. Be real. You'll be surprised what comes up when you give yourself permission to speak.

Writing is one of the most powerful tools for self-discovery. When you write without editing, without worrying about grammar or structure, you give yourself permission to be vulnerable. You tap into thoughts and emotions that are often buried, unspoken, and forgotten. This rawness will reveal things about yourself you didn't even realize were there. Don't be afraid to let your words flow freely. The more honest and real you are with yourself, the closer you'll get to understanding who you truly are—and what truly makes you feel alive.

You Are Allowed to Change

Change is often viewed with fear and resistance, but it's a natural and essential part of growth. We're constantly evolving, and that's exactly how it should be. The person you were a year ago isn't the person you are today, and the person you are today won't be the same a year from now. As you grow and gain new experiences, you'll begin to shed old versions of yourself—beliefs that no longer serve you, habits that limit you, and relationships that don't support the person you're becoming.

Self-discovery is not a destination. It's a lifelong journey.

You'll outgrow people. Beliefs. Habits. Even parts of yourself.

That's not inconsistency, it's evolution.

And the more you learn about who you are, the more you'll learn to love yourself fully, deeply, and honestly.

Let go of the fear of change. Allow yourself to grow and transform. You are allowed to change, and it's through this change that you'll find your truest, most complete self.

Your body holds truth your mind might ignore. Your body is always speaking. Start listening.

Chapter 9: You Are Not Alone
A Letter to Anyone Who's Still Healing

To the one who feels like they're behind,

To the one still carrying heartbreak quietly,

To the one healing from wounds no one else can see,

This is for you.

You don't have to be fully healed to be worthy of love.

You don't need to have it all figured out to deserve peace.

You are allowed to exist in the in-between, the messy middle, and still be proud of how far you've come.

Some days, you'll feel strong.

Other days, it will feel like the weight is back again, heavier than before. That's normal. Healing doesn't move in a straight line. It spirals. You revisit pain from different angles. But that doesn't mean you're back at the beginning.

Even your quietest progress still counts.

Even your invisible growth matters.

Remember, healing isn't about "fixing" yourself—it's about learning to embrace every part of you, even the broken parts. It's about giving yourself grace, knowing that it's okay to have bad days, and understanding that healing is a journey, not a race. You will emerge stronger, wiser, and more whole, even if it doesn't feel that way right now.

You Are Allowed to Take Your Time

We live in a world that moves fast. But your healing doesn't have to.

You are not late.

You are not falling behind.

You are simply moving at your own pace. And that pace is enough.

The world might tell you to rush, to keep up, to move faster, but your journey is uniquely yours. Your path may look different from others, and that's okay. It's not about comparing your progress to anyone else's—it's about honoring your own timeline.

Rest is not weakness.

Pauses are part of the progress.

The progress you're making, no matter how small it may seem, is progress. And it's leading you exactly where you need to go.

You Are So Much More Than What Hurt You

Yes, you've been hurt.

But you are not your pain.

It may leave scars, but it's the scars that show your resilience, your ability to endure, and your strength to keep going despite the challenges.

You are the way you got back up.

The kindness you still offer others.

The hope you keep holding onto, even if it's just a flicker.

There is so much life left in you. So much beauty. So much strength.

Even if today hurts, tomorrow holds possibility.

You are becoming more of who you are meant to be with every step, no matter how small. The life in you is still burning bright. The beauty of who you are is still unfolding, piece by piece. And no matter what has happened, you are worthy of everything good that's still to come.

So, don't give up on yourself, even when it feels hard. You are not defined by your pain. You are defined by your strength, your heart, and your unwavering belief that better days are ahead.

You Don't Have to Do This Alone

Please don't carry everything by yourself.

Talk to someone. A friend. A therapist. A journal. God. Your past self. Your future self.

Speak the weight out loud. Let someone help you hold it. There is strength in reaching out. You don't have to carry everything on your own. Too often, we convince ourselves that asking for help is a sign of weakness, or that we should be able to handle everything by ourselves. But the truth is, you don't have to face life's challenges alone.

Allow yourself to be supported, to feel seen, and to be heard. You deserve that. No one should have to go through their hardest moments in isolation. Let others be the shoulder you need to lean on, just as you would be for them.

You were never meant to walk this path alone.

A Reminder to Carry With You

There's no finish line you need to race toward.

Your healing is not a contest.

It's a quiet act of courage, done day by day, breath by breath.

You are doing better than you think.

And even if you don't feel it now, you are going to be okay.

You are allowed to be a work in progress and a masterpiece at the same time.

A Letter To You, The Reader

Dear You,

Thank you for walking through these pages with me.

Thank you for being brave enough to look inward, to feel deeply, and to begin again, even when it's hard. Especially when it's hard.

If no one has told you today: I'm proud of you.

For surviving. For healing. For choosing to keep going, even when the path was uncertain. I'm proud of you.

Healing is not a finish line.

Self-love isn't a perfect destination.

They are lifelong journeys. And you are allowed to travel them at your own pace.

Some days you'll rise strong. Other days you'll rest.

Both are part of the process.

Please remember this:

You are not broken.

You are not behind.

You are not alone.

You are still becoming. And that is a beautiful thing.

With warmth,

Sage Liberty

About the Author

Sage Liberty

Sage Liberty is a passionate writer from the Philippines, dedicated to inspiring and empowering others through her words. She believes in the power of storytelling to transform lives, and her mission is to help others realize their full potential. Liberty writes across multiple genres, including self-help, where she shares her and insights about overcoming adversity based on her experience and the others. Her writing journey began with a deep desire to guide others through their struggles, showing them that healing, growth, and self-discovery are within reach for anyone willing to embark on the journey.

Through her work, Liberty aims to show that no matter the challenges one faces, everyone has the power to heal, grow, and become the best version of themselves. She crafts relatable, authentic narratives that encourage her readers to reflect on their lives, take meaningful action, and embrace their true selves without fear. Drawing from her own life experiences and the stories of those she's encountered, Liberty's writing serves as a reminder that healing is possible, and transformation can start at any moment.

When she's not writing, Liberty enjoys quiet moments, indulging herself in watching anime and reading books that focus on self-discovery. These hobbies allow her to find inspiration and connect with the stories of others who are also navigating their paths to self-improvement. Liberty believes that the process of learning and growing is lifelong, and through her work, she hopes to offer both practical advice and emotional support to those seeking to better understand themselves.

Liberty is committed to helping others realize their worth and potential, one page at a time. Her writing is not only a reflection of her journey but a guide for others to walk confidently toward their own. Whether in her books or real life, she strives to remind them that they are capable of achieving greatness and becoming the person they've always wanted to be.

www.ingramcontent.com/pod-product-compliance
Lightning Source LLC
LaVergne TN
LVHW041640070526
838199LV00052B/3465